# Theseus and the Minotaur

### Ken Beatty

T0385989

## Level 1

Series Editors: Andy Hopkins and Jocelyn Potter

## 1.1 What's the book about?

Look at the picture on the front of this book. You can see a man and a Minotaur. Talk about the picture. Then write these words in the sentences.

| bad | dark | good | knife | room | name |
|-----|------|------|-------|------|------|

**1** They are in a small ..............room.............. .

**2** It is .............................. in the room.

**3** The young man's .............................. is Theseus.

**4** He is a .............................. man.

**5** The Minotaur is big and .............................. .

**6** The young man has a .............................. in his hand.

## 1.2 What happens first?

What do you think? Number the pictures, 1–4.

# CHAPTER 1

# A King's Sword

*'You have two fathers, Theseus,' his mother said. 'You are the son of Poseidon, the **god** of the sea, and the son of **King** Aegeus.'*

---

Theseus lived with his mother in Troezen, in Greece. He was a clever, happy young man, but he did not know his father.

One day, his mother said to him, 'Come with me into the garden, Theseus. Do you see that big **rock**? Can you move it, my son?'

Theseus was strong. He moved the rock and looked under it. There was a **sword** – a king's sword!

**god** /gɒd/ (n) Apollo was not a man. He was a Greek *god*.
**king** /kɪŋ/ (n) The people in this country love their *king*.
**rock** /rɒk/ (n) That *rock* is going to fall on his head.
**sword** /sɔːd/ (n) He was dead on the floor, with a *sword* in his back.

'This is the sword of King Aegeus,' his mother said. 'And now it is yours.'

Theseus looked at her, and then at the sword. 'Mine?' he said. 'Why is it mine?'

'You have two fathers, Theseus,' his mother said. 'You are the son of Poseidon, the god of the sea, and the son of King Aegeus. King Aegeus lives in Athens. Go to him now. It is time.'

That night, Theseus said goodbye to his mother.

'I am going to walk to my father's home,' he said to her.

'But it is a long and difficult walk,' his mother said.

'I am strong,' Theseus said. 'You know that, Mother. Don't **cry** for me.'

cry /kraɪ/ (v, past **cried** /kraɪd/) Don't *cry*! Be happy.

Theseus walked for ten days. There were many bad men on the road. But he **fought** them – and he **killed** them. Then he came to Athens, to the home of King Aegeus.

But Aegeus had a new **wife**, Medea, and she had a son too. She was angry about Theseus.

'He is your father's first son,' she said to her son. '*You* are going to be king after your father – not him.'

She wanted to kill Theseus. But Aegeus watched her and he stopped her.

The king talked to Theseus. 'You moved the rock and you have my sword,' he said. 'You are my son.'

**fight** /faɪt/ (v, past **fought** /fɔːt/) (n) Don't *fight* him! He has a knife.
**kill** /kɪl/ (v) They *kill* people for money.
**wife** /waɪf/ (n) My mother was my father's first *wife*.

# A King Cries

*'The Minotaur lives in a dark **maze** near its father's house.*
*People go into the maze – but they do not come out.'*

O ne evening, Theseus went for a walk in the garden. His father was there and he looked very unhappy.

'Why are you crying, Father?' Theseus asked.

'Early tomorrow a boat is going to **sail** to the **island** of Crete,' Aegeus said. 'Minos is king of Crete and his son is the Minotaur.'

'What is the Minotaur?' Theseus asked.

maze /meɪz/ (n) There are children in the *maze* and they can't get out.
sail /seɪl/ (v/n) I can *sail* those boats. The boats have white *sails*.
island /'aɪlənd/ (n) They are on holiday on one of the Caribbean *islands*.

4

'The Minotaur is **half bull** and half man. Minos had two sons, but we killed one in a fight. Then we **lost** the fight. Now, every year, fourteen young Athenians go to Crete. They are food for the Minotaur.'

'The Minotaur eats people?' Theseus asked.

'Yes,' his father said. 'The Minotaur lives in a dark maze near its father's house. People go into the maze – but they do not come out.'

Theseus was angry. 'Father,' he said. 'I can go too! I can fight the Minotaur! I can kill it!'

'How?' King Aegeus asked.

'I am strong and clever,' Theseus said. 'Tomorrow I am going to sail to the island of Crete!'

half /hɑːf/ (adj) He has got a *half* bottle of water.
bull /bʊl/ (n) The *bull* is a big black animal.
lose /luːz/ (v, past lost /lɒst/) I am angry because he *lost* my book.

## 2.1 Were you right?

Look at your answers to Activity 1.2 on page ii. Then circle the right answers.

| | | | |
|---|---|---|---|
| 1 | The sword is under a big rock. | Yes | **No** |
| 2 | Theseus can't move the rock. | Yes | **No** |
| 3 | It is Poseidon's sword. | Yes | **No** |
| 4 | Medea loves Theseus. | Yes | **No** |
| 5 | Theseus is King Aegeus's son. | Yes | **No** |

## 2.2 What more did you learn?

Write the names under the pictures. Then talk about the people. Are they good or bad?

King Aegeus   King Minos   Medea   Poseidon   Theseus

Medea's son   the Minotaur   Theseus's mother

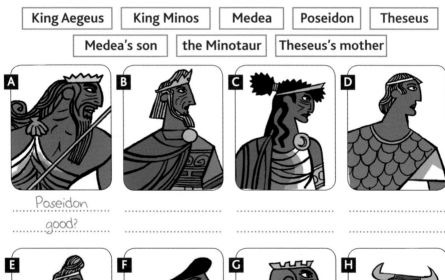

A ............Poseidon............
............good?............

B ............................

C ............................

D ............................

E ............................
............................

F ............................
............................

G ............................
............................

H ............................
............................

## 2.3 Language in use

**Look at the words on the right. Then put *going to* in the right place in these sentences.**

> 'Tomorrow I am **going to** sail to the island of Crete.'

**1** 'I am walk to my father's home.'

'I am going to walk to my father's home.'

**2** 'You are be king after your father.'

................................................................

**3** Medea's son is not be king.

................................................................

**4** Is the Minotaur eat the Athenians?

................................................................

**5** Theseus is to fight the Minotaur.

................................................................

## 2.4 What's next?

**What are you going to read now? Write ✓ or ✗.**

# CHAPTER 3

# A Lost Ring

*Ariadne looked at Theseus's beautiful face with love. She wanted to **help** him. She wanted to be his wife.*

'I am going to make a **promise** to you,' Theseus said to his father in the morning. 'I am going to come back again. Look at the sails of this boat. They are black. But we have white sails on the boat too. I am going to kill the Minotaur and we are going to come home again. Then our boat is going to have white sails. Watch for those white sails.'

'I am going to watch for them all day and all night,' King Aegeus said. 'Remember your promise!'

'The boat is going to sail now,' Theseus said. 'Goodbye, Father!'

help /help/ (v/n) She has got a problem. Please *help* her.
promise /ˈprɒmɪs/ (n/v) I am going to write to you every day. That's a *promise*.

The boat sailed quickly across the blue Aegean Sea to Crete.

King Minos and his daughter Ariadne waited for the boat. The young Athenians were very unhappy. Only one man did not cry.

'Who are you?' King Minos asked Theseus.

'I am Theseus,' he said. 'I am the son of King Aegeus. But I am the son of Poseidon, king of the sea, too.'

Minos smiled. 'You are the son of a god? What can you do? Let's see! My **ring** is in the sea. Swim down and find it for me!'

Theseus went into the water and asked for help. Two white **dolphin**s came to him with the ring.

'Here is your ring,' he said to King Minos.

Ariadne looked at Theseus's beautiful face with love. She wanted to help him. She wanted to be his wife.

Theseus and the Athenians went with the king's men. There was one small, dark room for Theseus and one room for the Athenians.

'The Minotaur had food today,' King Minos said. 'You can sleep.'

But the visitors did not sleep.

ring /rɪŋ/ (n) The girls have beautiful *rings* on their hands.
dolphin /'dɒlfɪn/ (n) *Dolphins* swim near the boats.

# CHAPTER 4

# A Woman's Help

*'The Minotaur is sleeping now,' Theseus said. 'I am going to kill it before morning.*
*Then we can all go back to Athens.'*

---

That evening, Ariadne went to Theseus's room.
'I want to talk to him,' she said to the men at the door. The men opened the door for her.

Under her dress she had a knife and some **string**. 'Take these,' she said quietly to Theseus. 'Kill the Minotaur with the knife. But it is very dark in the maze. Put one **end** of the string under a rock near the door. Then take the string into the maze with you.'

string /strıŋ/ (n) Close the bag with some *string*.
end /end/ (n) We walk to the school at the *end* of the road.

'Why are you helping me?' Theseus asked.

'I don't like my father,' Ariadne said. 'And I don't like Crete. Kill the Minotaur, but take me away with you. Promise!'

'I promise,' Theseus said.

He did not want to wait for the morning.

'The Minotaur is sleeping now,' Theseus said. 'I am going to kill it before morning. Then we can all go back to Athens. Please, Ariadne, help my friends. Take the young Athenians to the boat.'

'Yes,' said Ariadne, and she went.

First, Theseus killed the two men at the door with his knife. Then he went to the Minotaur's maze.

## 3.1 Were you right?

**Look at your answers to Activity 2.4 on page 7. Then write the words in the sentences.**

> waits   loves   help   sails   eat   sail

**1** Theseus and the young Athenians .......................... to Crete.

**2** Their boat has black .......................... .

**3** Ariadne .......................... Theseus.

**4** She wants to .......................... him.

**5** The Minotaur doesn't .......................... any Athenians that day.

**6** Theseus .......................... in a small, dark room.

## 3.2 What more did you learn?

**Who is talking?**

**1** 'I am going to come back again.'

**2** 'Remember your promise!'

**3** 'My ring is in the sea.'

**4** 'You can sleep.'

**5** 'Kill the Minotaur with the knife.'

**6** 'Take the young Athenians to the boat.'

## 3.3 Language in use

**Look at the words on the right. Then write** *promise* **or** *promised* **in these sentences.**

> 'I am going to make a **promise** to you.'
>
> 'I **promise**.'

1  'Remember your ........promise........ !'

2  'Kill the Minotaur, but take me away with you. ............................. !'

3  'I am going to kill the Minotaur. I ............................ my father.'

4  She is going to sail away from Crete. That is Theseus's ............................
   to her.

5  What did Theseus ............................ Ariadne?

6  Ariadne is happy because Theseus ............................ .

## 3.4 What's next?

**Look at the pictures. What are these people going to do? Write sentences.**

.........................................................     .........................................................
.........................................................     .........................................................

.........................................................     .........................................................
.........................................................     .........................................................

# CHAPTER 5

# The End of the Minotaur

*The Minotaur's eyes opened and it moved quickly. Suddenly,
Theseus was on the floor.*

---

Theseus arrived at the door to the Minotaur's maze. It was very
dark, but Theseus remembered the string. He started it at the door
of the maze. Then he walked slowly into the maze and listened for the
Minotaur.

There was no noise.

Theseus walked and walked in the cold, dark maze. The end of the string was always in his hand.

And then he sees it – the Minotaur! His hand goes to his knife and the string falls to the floor. But his foot hits a small rock. The Minotaur's eyes open at the noise and it moves quickly. Suddenly, Theseus is on the floor.

But Theseus is young and strong and he has his knife. Again and again, his knife goes into the Minotaur's head. It is a long and difficult fight. But in the end the Minotaur is on the floor.

It is dead.

But it was very dark in the maze. Where was the door? Theseus remembered the string. He walked back to the door and then to the boat – and there were Ariadne and the young Athenians.

'Quickly!' Theseus said. 'The Minotaur is dead. Let's sail for Athens!'

'Theseus, remember your promise!' Ariadne said. 'Take me with you!'

Theseus, Ariadne and the young Athenians sailed for Athens, but first the boat stopped at the island of Naxos.

'You cannot go to Athens with us,' Theseus said to Ariadne. 'Please get off here.'

'But I want to go to Athens!' Ariadne cried. 'I love you and I want to be your wife!'

'I did not promise you that,' Theseus said. 'You wanted to get away from Crete. You can live here.'

'Theseus, you promised!' Ariadne said. She was very angry. 'Now *you* are going to be very unhappy too.'

# CHAPTER 6

# Black Sails, White Sails

*'The sails!' Theseus suddenly said. 'Take down the black sails
and put up the white sails!'*

---

Theseus and the young Athenians sailed home to Athens. They talked about Theseus's fight with the Minotaur and they were very happy. They did not talk about Ariadne. She was the daughter of King Minos. They did not want her on their boat.

They sailed all day and watched the white dolphins in the sea near the boat. In the evening, the lights of Athens were in front of them. They all smiled.

'The sails!' Theseus suddenly said. 'Take down the black sails and put up the white sails! I promised my father. Do it quickly, or he is not going to know about the Minotaur.'

The white sails went up, but the boat was very near Athens.

The same day, King Aegeus was in his garden. He watched the sea. There was the boat! And there were the black sails!

'Oh, Theseus, my son, did the Minotaur kill you?' he cried.

A short time later, Aegeus was dead.

Theseus and his boat arrived in Athens. The people of Athens were happy because their children were home again. But they were very unhappy about the old king. Theseus was unhappy too. He was the killer of the Minotaur and the new King of Athens – but he cried for his father.

19

## Work with a friend. Ask and answer these questions.

Why did I send Theseus to Crete?

Why is Ariadne in our boat?

Why am I on Naxos?

Why didn't I remember my promise?

Why did Theseus kill me?

Why isn't my son king?

Why is Theseus in Athens again?

You are Ariadne. Now you live on Naxos. Are you angry? Do you have questions? Write a letter to Theseus.

**1** **Answer the questions.**

**1** Who did Theseus make a promise to?

**2** What was the promise?

**3** Did he do it?

**4** What do you think? Was he right?

**2** **Who is right? Why? Read the words and talk to your friends.**

| A | B | C |
|---|---|---|
| Promises are not important. They're only words. | You make a promise, then you do it. | Some promises are important. Some promises are not. |

**3** **Who do we make promises to? And what do we say? Look at these pictures. Write the promises.**

I'm going to love you for all time. I promise.

He did it!

............................
............................

What's this?

............................
............................

Don't be late!

............................
............................

**4** Are you an angry person? Do you get up late? Do you watch TV for a long time every evening? Now is the time! Be a new person! Write your promises in the box. Here are some words for your promises.

| angry | early | late | well | cry | fight | hit | make | money |
|-------|-------|------|------|-----|-------|-----|------|-------|

| get a job | start work | watch TV | visit | go for a run |
|-----------|------------|----------|-------|--------------|

### THE NEW ME!

I'm not going to get angry with people.

**5** Now talk to your friends about your promises. In one week, look again at a friend's promises. Did he/she do well?